Let's Look at Strawberries

Katie Peters

GRL Consultants,
Diane Craig and Monica Marx,
Certified Literacy Specialists

Pull Ahead READERS

Lerner Publications ◆ Minneapolis

Note from a GRL Consultant
This Pull Ahead leveled book has been carefully designed for beginning readers. A team of guided reading literacy experts has reviewed and leveled the book to ensure readers pull ahead and experience success.

Lerner Publications Company
An imprint of Lerner Publishing Group, Inc.
241 First Avenue North
Minneapolis, MN 55401 USA

For reading levels and more information, look up this title at www.lernerbooks.com.

Main body text set in Memphis Pro 24/39
Typeface provided by Linotype.

Photo Acknowledgments
The images in this book are used with the permission of: © anna1311/iStockphoto, p. 3; © elf911/iStockphoto, pp. 4, 5, 16 (seeds); © Ipinchuk/iStockphoto, pp. 8, 9; © Ixta/iStockphoto, pp. 14, 15; © kiankhoon/iStockphoto, pp. 12, 13; © Neyya/iStockphoto, pp. 6, 7, 16 (flowers, plants); © romiri/iStockphoto, pp. 10, 11, 16 (strawberries).

Front cover: © YuriyS/iStockphoto

Library of Congress Cataloging-in-Publication Data

Names: Peters, Katie, author.
Title: Let's look at strawberries / Katie Peters.
Description: Minneapolis : Lerner Publications, [2021] | Series: Plant life cycles (pull ahead readers - nonfiction) | Includes index. | Audience: Ages 4–7 | Audience: Grades K–1 | Summary: "Sweet and fragrant, strawberries start as seeds and grow into the well-loved, bright red fruit. Vibrant photos and carefully leveled text show readers the strawberry life cycle. Pairs with the fiction title Sharing Berries."— Provided by publisher.
Identifiers: LCCN 2019045814 (print) | LCCN 2019045815 (ebook) | ISBN 9781541590236 (library binding) | ISBN 9781728403151 (paperback) | ISBN 9781728400778 (ebook)
Subjects: LCSH: Strawberries—Life cycles—Juvenile literature.
Classification: LCC SB385 .P48 2021 (print) | LCC SB385 (ebook) | DDC 634/.75—dc23

LC record available at https://lccn.loc.gov/2019045814
LC ebook record available at https://lccn.loc.gov/2019045815

Manufactured in the United States of America
4-1008976-48077-5/29/2024

Contents

Let's Look at Strawberries

Strawberry plants grow from seeds.
The seeds are tiny.

Flowers grow from
the plants.
The flowers are white.

Berries grow from
the flowers.
The berries are green.

The berries grow bigger.
They turn red.

I pick the berries.

I eat the berries.

Do you see the seeds on the berry?

Did You See It?

berries

strawberry flowers

strawberry plants

strawberry seeds

Index